# MATH PRACTICE

New York • Toronto • London • Auckland • Sydney
Mexico City • New Delhi • Hong Kong • Buenos Aires

Teaching Resources

Cover design by Jay Namerow
Interior illustrations by Jon Buller, Micheal Denman, Reggie Holladay, Susan Hendron, Jared Lee, Kathy Marlin, Bob Masheris, Mark Mason, and Mike Moran
Interior design by Quack & Company

ISBN 0-439-81917-2

4 5 6 7 8 9 10  08  13 12 11 10

# Table of Contents

Dear Parent:

Welcome to *3rd Grade Math Practice!* This valuable tool is designed to help your child succeed in school. Scholastic, the most trusted name in learning, has been creating quality educational materials for school and home for nearly a century. And this resource is no exception.

Inside this book, you'll find colorful and engaging activity pages that will give your child the practice he or she needs to master essential skills, such as adding and subtracting, multiplying, graphing, identifying fractions, and so much more.

To support your child's learning experience at home, try these helpful tips:

- Provide a comfortable, well-lit place to work, making sure your child has all the supplies he or she needs.

- Encourage your child to work at his or her own pace. Children learn at different rates and will naturally develop skills in their own time.

- Praise your child's efforts. If your child makes a mistake, offer words of encouragement and positive help.

- Display your child's work and celebrate his successes with family and friends.

We hope you and your child will enjoy working together to complete this workbook.

Happy learning!
The Editors

# Newspaper Math

## What to Do:

Use a newspaper to find the numbers listed below. Cut out your answers from the newspaper and tape them in the box with each question.

1. **From the weather report, find the temperature in two cities.**

2. **Pick three items advertised for sale.**

3. **Find two different times that the same movie is playing.**

4. **From the TV listings, pick three programs that you would like to watch. Include the channels that those programs will be on.**

5. **Choose two numbers from an article of your choice.**

# Place-Value Puzzler

## What is too much fun for one, enough for two, and means nothing to three?

Find the answer to this riddle by using place value! Take a look at each number below. One digit in each number is underlined. Circle the word in each line that tells the place value of the underlined number. Write the letters next to each correct answer in the blanks below. The first one is done for you.

| | | | | |
|---|---|---|---|---|
| **A.** | 1<u>5</u>,209 | **a** thousands | **i** hundreds |
| **B.** | 4,7<u>2</u>9 | **n** hundreds | **s** tens |
| **C.** | <u>4</u>25 | **e** hundreds | **o** tens |
| **D.** | 7,6<u>1</u>8 | **c** tens | **g** ones |
| **E.** | 1,<u>1</u>12 | **p** thousands | **r** hundreds |
| **F.** | 8,63<u>6</u> | **a** hundreds | **e** ones |
| **G.** | 2<u>2</u>2 | **t** tens | **m** ones |

$\underset{\text{A}}{a}$ __ __ __ __ __ __
     B     C     D     E     F     G

# Bee Riddle

**Riddle: What did the farmer get when he tried to reach the beehive?**

Round each number. Then use the Decoder to solve the riddle by filling in the spaces at the bottom of the page.

**Decoder**

| | |
|---|---|
| 400 | A |
| 800 | W |
| 30 | O |
| 10 | Y |
| 25 | E |
| 500 | I |
| 210 | J |
| 20 | L |
| 40 | C |
| 700 | U |
| 90 | S |
| 100 | T |
| 600 | G |
| 95 | F |
| 50 | N |
| 550 | V |
| 300 | Z |
| 7 | H |
| 200 | Z |

**1** Round 7 to the nearest ten     _____

**2** Round 23 to the nearest ten     _____

**3** Round 46 to the nearest ten     _____

**4** Round 92 to the nearest ten     _____

**5** Round 203 to the nearest hundred _____

**6** Round 420 to the nearest hundred_____

**7** Round 588 to the nearest hundred_____

**8** Round 312 to the nearest hundred_____

**9** Round 549 to the nearest hundred_____

**10** Round 710 to the nearest hundred_____

A "B\_\_ \_\_ \_\_ \_\_ " \_\_ \_\_ \_\_ \_\_ \_\_ \_\_
    10  5  8  1    4  9  7  3  6  2

# Great States

Add or subtract. Connect the matching answers
to find each state's shape.

| | |
|---|---|
| Delaware | **16 – 9 =** |
| Massachusetts | **7 + 7 =** |
| New Hampshire | **15 – 6 =** |
| New York | **17 + 1 =** |
| South Carolina | **14 – 3 =** |
| Maryland | **15 – 2 =** |
| Pennsylvania | **14 – 9 =** |
| Connecticut | **12 + 5 =** |
| Rhode Island | **7 + 3 =** |
| North Carolina | **13 – 7 =** |
| Georgia | **7 + 5 =** |
| New Jersey | **14 – 6 =** |
| Virginia | **7 + 8 =** |

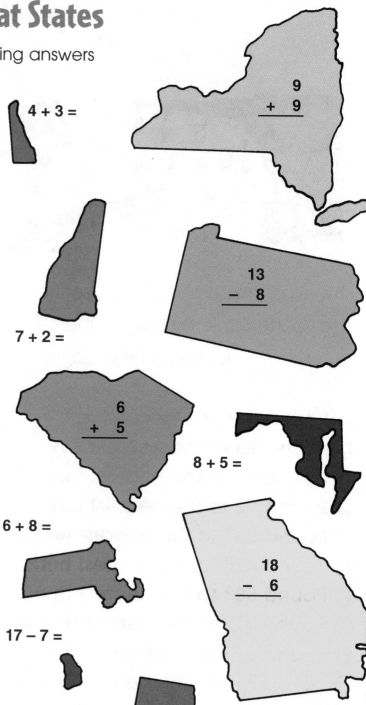

$4 + 3 =$

$$\begin{array}{r} 9 \\ +\ 9 \\ \hline \end{array}$$

$$\begin{array}{r} 13 \\ -\ 8 \\ \hline \end{array}$$

$7 + 2 =$

$$\begin{array}{r} 6 \\ +\ 5 \\ \hline \end{array}$$

$8 + 5 =$

$6 + 8 =$

$$\begin{array}{r} 18 \\ -\ 6 \\ \hline \end{array}$$

$17 - 7 =$

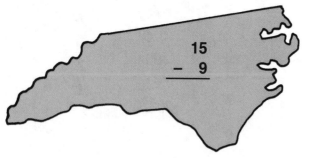

$$\begin{array}{r} 15 \\ -\ 9 \\ \hline \end{array}$$

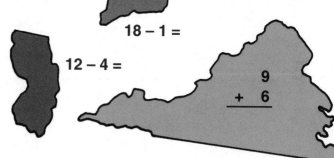

$18 - 1 =$

$12 - 4 =$

$$\begin{array}{r} 9 \\ +\ 6 \\ \hline \end{array}$$

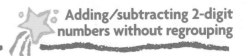

# United We Stand

Add or subtract. Color answers greater than 50 green to show the United States.
Color answers less than 50 blue.

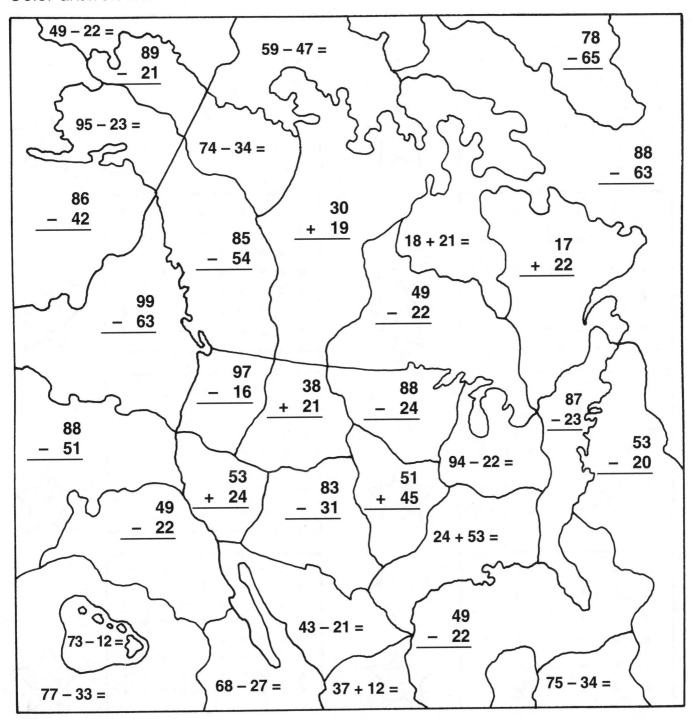

49 – 22 =

89
– 21

59 – 47 =

78
– 65

95 – 23 =

74 – 34 =

88
– 63

86
– 42

85
– 54

30
+ 19

18 + 21 =

17
+ 22

99
– 63

49
– 22

97
– 16

38
+ 21

88
– 24

87
– 23

88
– 51

53
– 20

53
+ 24

83
– 31

51
+ 45

94 – 22 =

49
– 22

24 + 53 =

73 – 12 =

49
– 22

43 – 21 =

77 – 33 =

68 – 27 =

37 + 12 =

75 – 34 =

**Can you find Hawaii in the map above? Write an addition problem that has the
same answer.**

# Stars and Stripes Forever

Circle groups of 10. Write the number of tens and ones. Write the number in the star.

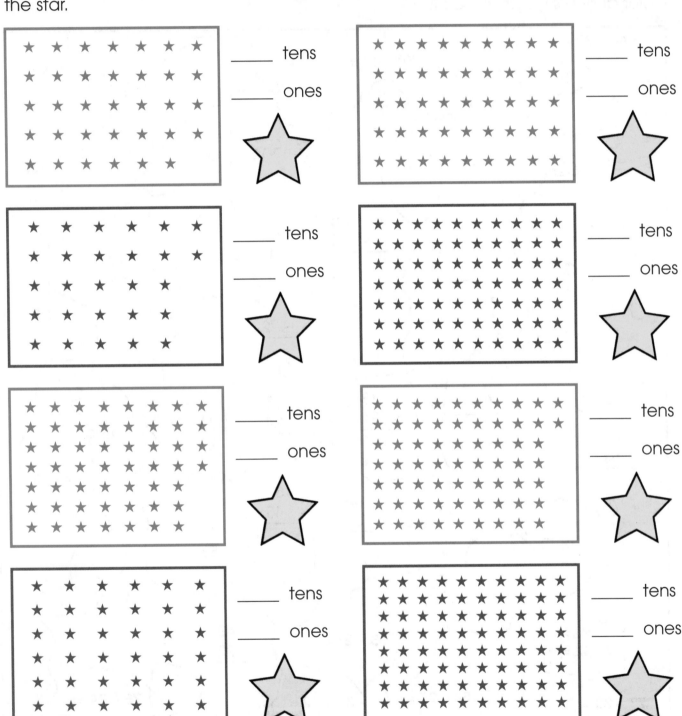

_____ tens

_____ ones

_____ tens

_____ ones

_____ tens

_____ ones

_____ tens

_____ ones

_____ tens

_____ ones

_____ tens

_____ ones

_____ tens

_____ ones

_____ tens

_____ ones

 **Find out how many stars were on the first flag. On another piece of paper, add that number to the number of stars on the United States flag today. How many groups of tens and ones are there?**

# Mr. President

Add. Write the letters in the circles to identify each president.

### I was a leader in the Civil War.

| 39<br>+ 13 | 38<br>+ 15 | 56<br>+ 26 | 26<br>+ 35 | 29<br>+ 67 | 27<br>+ 25 | 43<br>+ 39 |
|---|---|---|---|---|---|---|
|  |  |  |  |  |  |  |

◯ ◯ ◯ ◯ ◯ ◯ ◯

### I helped write the Declaration of Independence.

| 19<br>+ 18 | 28<br>+ 55 | 24<br>+ 18 | 19<br>+ 23 | 17<br>+ 66 | 59<br>+ 19 | 49<br>+ 15 | 78<br>+ 18 | 48<br>+ 34 |
|---|---|---|---|---|---|---|---|---|
|  |  |  |  |  |  |  |  |  |

◯ ◯ ◯ ◯ ◯ ◯ ◯ ◯ ◯

### I was a leader in the American Revolutionary War.

| 59<br>+ 39 | 48<br>+ 24 | 27<br>+ 37 | 19<br>+ 46 | 27<br>+ 26 | 38<br>+ 44 | 27<br>+ 18 | 18<br>+ 29 | 38<br>+ 58 | 27<br>+ 55 |
|---|---|---|---|---|---|---|---|---|---|
|  |  |  |  |  |  |  |  |  |  |

◯ ◯ ◯ ◯ ◯ ◯ ◯ ◯ ◯ ◯

### Code

| 61 C | 98 W | 55 Y | 83 E | 45 G | 82 N | 78 R | 65 H | 52 L |
|---|---|---|---|---|---|---|---|---|
| 96 O | 42 F | 86 K | 47 T | 72 A | 37 J | 64 S | 53 I | 36 D |

**On another piece of paper, make a code and write problems for the name of our current president.**

# Travel the Nation

Look at the number on each form of transportation. Write the number of tens and ones. Regroup. Write the new number.

Trade 1 ten for 10 ones.

37 — _3_ tens _7_ ones — _2_ tens _17_ ones

52 — ___ tens ___ ones — Trade 1 ten for 10 ones. — ___ tens ___ ones

85 — ___ tens ___ ones — Trade 1 ten for 10 ones. — ___ tens ___ ones

43 — ___ tens ___ ones — Trade 1 ten for 10 ones. — ___ tens ___ ones

68 — ___ tens ___ ones — Trade 1 ten for 10 ones. — ___ tens ___ ones

26 — ___ tens ___ ones — Trade 1 ten for 10 ones. — ___ tens ___ ones

# Great Vacations

Subtract. Draw a line from each difference to the vacation spot on the map.

| Mount Rushmore | Niagara Falls | Gateway Arch | Four Corners Monument | Statue of Liberty |
|---|---|---|---|---|
| 72<br>− 27 | 57<br>− 29 | 58<br>− 39 | 93<br>− 19 | 94<br>− 29 |

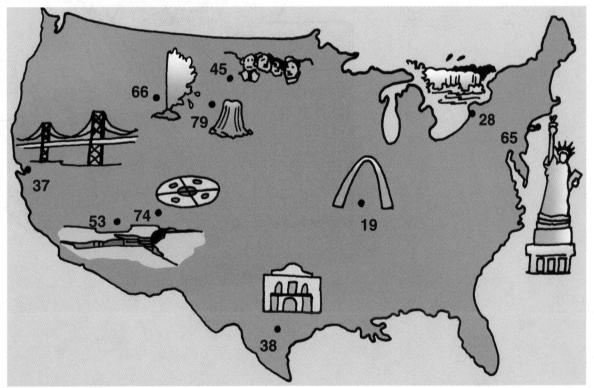

| Grand Canyon | Devil's Tower | Golden Gate Bridge | The Alamo | Old Faithful |
|---|---|---|---|---|
| 82<br>− 29 | 93<br>− 14 | 64<br>− 27 | 66<br>− 28 | 94<br>− 28 |

On the map above, mark and write the name of a vacation spot in the United States you would like to visit. Write a subtraction problem for it.

# Great Math Inventions

Add or subtract. Then write the problem's letter above its matching answer below

S.  29
  + 46

I.  48
  − 24

A.  27
  + 38

R.  56
  − 18

R.  37
  + 47

W.  81
  − 24

H.  23
  + 35

I.  90
  − 26

U.  52
  − 19

O.  37
  + 35

L.  70
  − 19

M.  82
  − 48

B.  23
  + 48

L.  52
  + 28

G.  91
  − 22

U.  73
  − 25

___ ___ ___ ___ ___ ___ ___    ___ ___ ___ ___ ___ ___ ___ ___ ___
57  24  80  51  64  65  34     71  48  84  38  72  33  69  58  75

**invented and patented the adding machine in St. Louis, Missouri, in 1888.**

# It All Adds Up!

Add. Fill in the missing numbers.

```
   3  2  4          2  4 □          □  5  5         2 □  3
+  6  3 □       +  □  5  1       +  3 □  1       + □  1  3
----------      ----------      ----------      ----------
 □ □  6          7 □  2          4  8 □          5  2 □


   4  1 □          □  4  3          2 □ □          □  3  1
+  3 □  2       +  1  4 □       +  2  1  6       +  4 □ □
----------      ----------      ----------      ----------
 □  3  7          2 □  9          □  1  8          8  5  3


   1 □  2          □  4  1          3  3 □          □  1  2
+ □  3  3       +  1  3 □       + □ □  3       +  2 □  2
----------      ----------      ----------      ----------
   3  7 □          6 □  5          6  6  8          9  4 □


   2  2 □          5 □  4          2  2  4          □  1  6
+  3  1  4      + □  3  4       +  1 □  3       +  1  3 □
----------      ----------      ----------      ----------
 □ □  4          8  4 □         □  6 □          5 □  8
```

💡 Joe and Ellie were going to the movies. Joe brought $5.□0, and Ellie brought $□.35. If they had $9.75 altogether, how much money did they each have? Show your work.

# A, B, C, . . .

Add.

**K F J A H I D B L C E M G**

| | | |
|---|---|---|
| 286<br>+ 668 | 138<br>+ 289 | 285<br>+ 269 |
| 496<br>+ 188 | 159<br>+ 190 | 175<br>+ 189 |
| 499<br>+ 446 | 375<br>+ 469 | 183<br>+ 289 |
| 299<br>+ 158 | 196<br>+ 378 | 657<br>+ 285 |
| 186<br>+ 287 | 157<br>+ 267 | 276<br>+ 566 |

| | | |
|---|---|---|
| 295<br>+ 675 | 188<br>+ 185 | 487<br>+ 385 |
| 284<br>+ 439 | 389<br>+ 188 | 595<br>+ 289 |
| 128<br>+ 379 | 297<br>+ 179 | 198<br>+ 199 |
| 365<br>+ 378 | 192<br>+ 579 | 123<br>+ 589 |
| 386<br>+ 189 | 295<br>+ 379 | 436<br>+ 538 |

This letter sounds like a question.

Color each answer with a 4 in the ones place to see!

This letter names a feature on your fac

Color each answer with a 7 in the tens place to see!

Add.

## . . . X, Y, and Z

| | | |
|---|---|---|
| 298<br>+ 276 | 191<br>+ 343 | 269<br>+ 289 |
| 157<br>+ 189 | 137<br>+ 369 | 278<br>+ 485 |
| 395<br>+ 457 | 244<br>+ 279 | 499<br>+ 446 |
| 288<br>+ 664 | 236<br>+ 288 | 577<br>+ 388 |
| 498<br>+ 399 | 399<br>+ 164 | 284<br>+ 439 |

| | | |
|---|---|---|
| 259<br>+ 467 | 364<br>+ 258 | 487<br>+ 436 |
| 199<br>+ 128 | 199<br>+ 89 | 238<br>+ 287 |
| 255<br>+ 373 | 509<br>+ 315 | 117<br>+ 314 |
| 257<br>+ 569 | 276<br>+ 566 | 149<br>+ 279 |
| 339<br>+ 385 | 258<br>+ 467 | 179<br>+ 348 |

This letter names an icy drink.

Color each answer with a 5 in the hundreds place to see!

This letter names an insect that stings.

Color each answer with a 2 in the tens place to see!

# Let's Talk

Find the number that goes with
each letter on the phone. Subtract.

| | |
|---|---|
| J D H <br> – A P L | – |

| | |
|---|---|
| G M Q <br> – C S V | – |

| | |
|---|---|
| E W A <br> – B Y N | – |

Phone keypad:
1  ABC 2  DEF 3
GHI 4  JKL 5  MNO 6
PQRS 7  TUV 8  WXYZ 9

| | |
|---|---|
| M A L <br> – F N O | – |

| | |
|---|---|
| W T U <br> – J V W | – |

| | |
|---|---|
| R E K <br> – D M P | – |

| | |
|---|---|
| T J I <br> – E X Q | – |

| | |
|---|---|
| K N H <br> – H Z U | – |

| | |
|---|---|
| F D X <br> – B G Y | – |

**Find the numbers for your name. Add to find the sum of the numbers.**

# Home Sweet Home

Use the coordinates to find each number. Add or subtract.

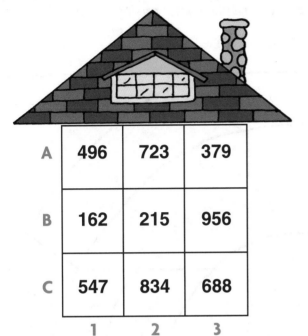

|   | 1 | 2 | 3 |
|---|---|---|---|
| A | 496 | 723 | 379 |
| B | 162 | 215 | 956 |
| C | 547 | 834 | 688 |

|   | 4 | 5 | 6 |
|---|---|---|---|
| E | 668 | 884 | 345 |
| F | 239 | 716 | 188 |
| G | 422 | 578 | 957 |

**A.** (A, 1)
(F, 6)  − _____

**B.** (B, 3)
(E, 4)  − _____

**C.** (C, 1)
(F, 4)  + _____

**D.** (A, 3)
(E, 6)  + _____

**E.** (A, 2)
(B, 1)  − _____

**F.** (G, 4)
(B, 2)  − _____

**G.** (G, 6)
(C, 3)  − _____

**H.** (E, 5)
(C, 2)  + _____

**I.** (B, 3)
(G, 5)  − _____

 **Color the largest number on each house orange. Color the smallest number on each house purple.**

# Code Zero! Code One!

 *When a number is multiplied by 0, the product is always 0.*
*When a number is multiplied by 1, the product is always the number being multiplied.*

Multiply. Shade all products of 0 yellow. Shade all other products green.

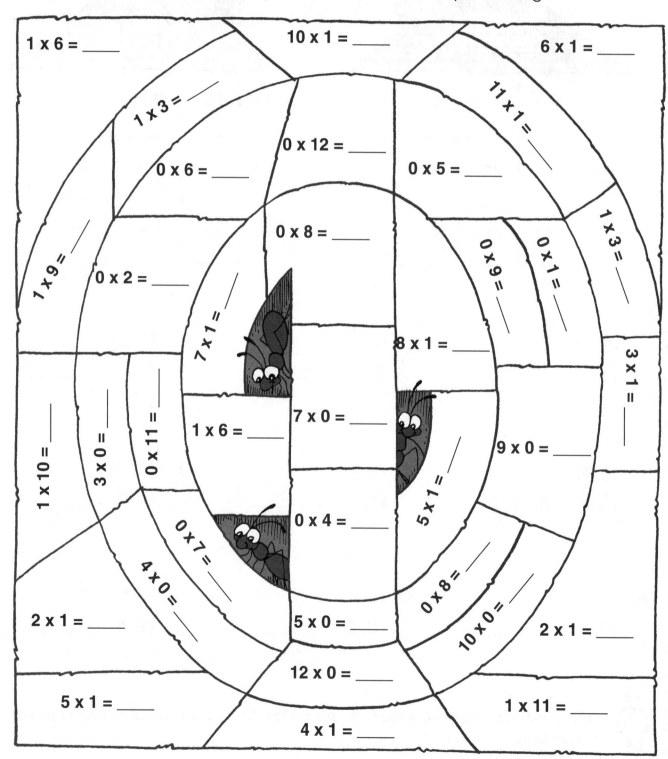

1 x 6 = _____    10 x 1 = _____    6 x 1 = _____

1 x 3 = _____    11 x 1 = _____

0 x 12 = _____

0 x 6 = _____    0 x 5 = _____

0 x 8 = _____

1 x 9 = _____    0 x 2 = _____    0 x 9 = _____    0 x 1 = _____    1 x 3 = _____

7 x 1 = _____    8 x 1 = _____    3 x 1 = _____

1 x 10 = _____    3 x 0 = _____    0 x 11 = _____    1 x 6 = _____    7 x 0 = _____    9 x 0 = _____

5 x 1 = _____

0 x 7 = _____    0 x 4 = _____

4 x 0 = _____    0 x 8 = _____

2 x 1 = _____    5 x 0 = _____    10 x 0 = _____    2 x 1 = _____

12 x 0 = _____

5 x 1 = _____    4 x 1 = _____    1 x 11 = _____

# Two, Four, Six, Eight, Who Do We

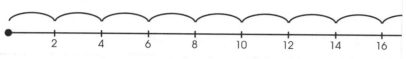

*When multiplying by 2, skip count by 2, or think of number line j*

Multiply.

**A.** 2 x 3 = \_\_\_\_     2 x 8 = \_\_\_\_     11 x 2 = \_\_\_\_     2 x 7 = \_\_\_\_

**B.** 8 x 2 = \_\_\_\_     4 x 2 = \_\_\_\_     2 x 2 = \_\_\_\_     2 x 4 = \_\_\_\_

**C.** 12 x 2 = \_\_\_\_     5 x 2 = \_\_\_\_     10 x 2 = \_\_\_\_     2 x 12 = \_\_\_\_

**D.** 9 x 2 = \_\_\_\_     2 x 1 = \_\_\_\_     2 x 10 = \_\_\_\_     7 x 2 = \_\_\_\_

**E.** 2 x 0 = \_\_\_\_     2 x 6 = \_\_\_\_     3 x 2 = \_\_\_\_     0 x 2 = \_\_\_\_

**F.** 2 x 5 = \_\_\_\_     2 x 9 = \_\_\_\_

**G.** 6 x 2 = \_\_\_\_     1 x 2 = \_\_\_\_

**H.** 2 x 11 = \_\_\_\_     2 x 2 = \_\_\_\_

**On another piece of paper, write a rhyme to go with each multiplication fact for 2.**
**Examples: "2 x 4 = 8, I love math, can you relate?" Or, "2 x 4 = 8, I've got to go and shut the gate!"**

# A Positive Answer

## What should you say if you are asked, "Do you want to learn the 3s?"

To find out, look at each problem below. If the product is correct, color the space green. If the product is incorrect, color the space yellow.

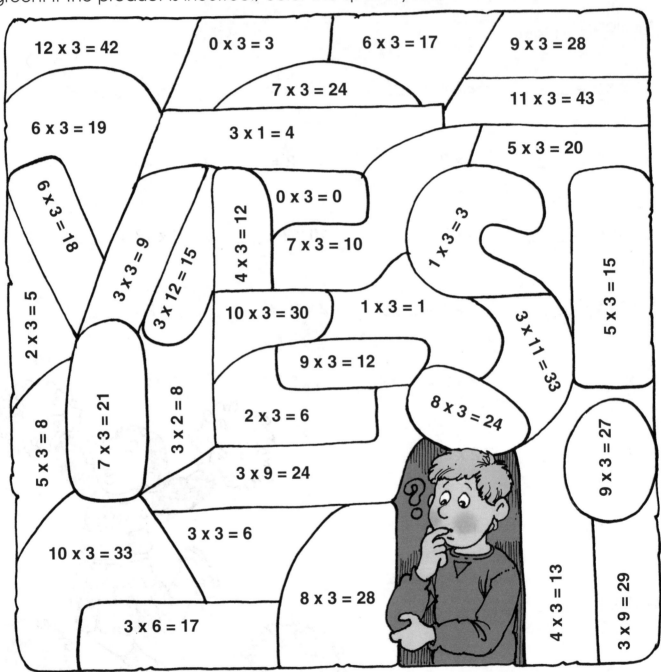

How many letters are in the answer to the puzzle? If you wrote this word ten times, how many letters would you write altogether?

# Puzzling Facts

Multiply. Write the number word for each product in the puzzle. Don't forget the hyphens!

**Across**

2. 4 x 9 = _____

4. 4 x 5 = _____

7. 4 x 3 = _____

8. 4 x 7 = _____

9. 4 x 10 = _____

11. 4 x 0 = _____

12. 4 x 11 = _____

**Down**

1. 4 x 4 = _____

2. 4 x 8 = _____

3. 4 x 12 = _____

5. 4 x 2 = _____

6. 4 x 6 = _____

10. 4 x 1 = _____

 **Tracy was missing 4 buttons on 11 different shirts. How many buttons does she need to fix all the shirts?**

# How Many Can You Find?

Complete each multiplication sentence. Then circle each answer in the picture.

**A.** 2 x 5 = _____

**B.** 5 x _____ = 5

**C.** _____ x 5 = 35

**D.** 10 x 5 = _____

**E.** _____ x 5 = 60

**F.** 5 x 6 = _____

**G.** _____ x 5 = 55

**H.** 5 x 3 = _____

**I.** 8 x 5 = _____

**J.** _____ x 5 = 45

**K.** 2 x _____ = 10

**L.** _____ x 5 = 25

**M.** 7 x 5 = _____

**N.** 5 x 12 = _____

**O.** 5 x _____ = 20

 **Squeaky Squirrel lived in a tree with 4 squirrel friends. If each squirrel collected 12 nuts, how many nuts altogether did the squirrels collect?**

# Mathematics Fireworks

Multiply. On another piece of paper, find the sum of the products of each star trail. Then use the key to color each star to match its star trail sum.

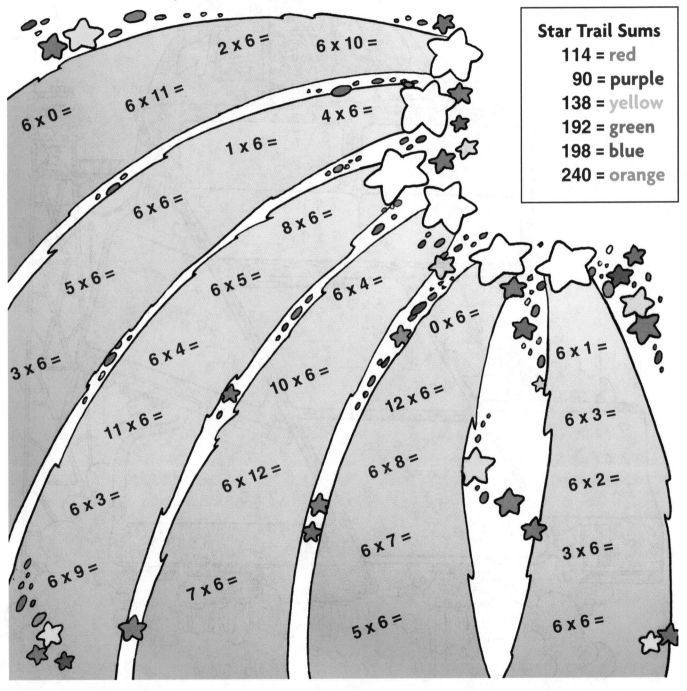

**Star Trail Sums**
114 = red
90 = purple
138 = yellow
192 = green
198 = blue
240 = orange

2 x 6 =
6 x 10 =
6 x 0 =
6 x 11 =
4 x 6 =
1 x 6 =
6 x 6 =
8 x 6 =
5 x 6 =
6 x 5 =
6 x 4 =
3 x 6 =
6 x 4 =
0 x 6 =
6 x 1 =
11 x 6 =
10 x 6 =
12 x 6 =
6 x 3 =
6 x 3 =
6 x 12 =
6 x 8 =
6 x 2 =
6 x 9 =
6 x 7 =
3 x 6 =
7 x 6 =
5 x 6 =
6 x 6 =

**Emma counted the fireworks she watched on the Fourth of July. She counted 6 different fireworks every 15 minutes. The firework show lasted 2 hours. How many fireworks did Emma see?**

# Flying Sevens

Multiply.

$7 \times 9 =$ _____

$11 \times 7 =$ _____

$6 \times 7 =$ _____

$7 \times 4 =$ _____

$3 \times 7 =$ _____

$7 \times 7 =$ _____

$7 \times 10 =$ _____

$7 \times 0 =$ _____

$5 \times 7 =$ _____

$7 \times 12 =$ _____

$7 \times 2 =$ _____

$4 \times 7 =$ _____

$7 \times 11 =$ _____

$1 \times 7 =$ _____

$0 \times 7 =$ _____

$7 \times 8 =$ _____

$2 \times 7 =$ _____

$7 \times 1 =$ _____

$7 \times 6 =$ _____

$8 \times 7 =$ _____

$9 \times 7 =$ _____

$10 \times 7 =$ _____

$12 \times 7 =$ _____

$7 \times 3 =$ _____

$7 \times 5 =$ _____

 **Cassandra's space mission is to orbit Earth seven times as quickly as she can a total of seven times. How many times altogether will she orbit Earth?**

# The Ultimate Eight Track

Use a stopwatch to time how long it takes to multiply around the track.

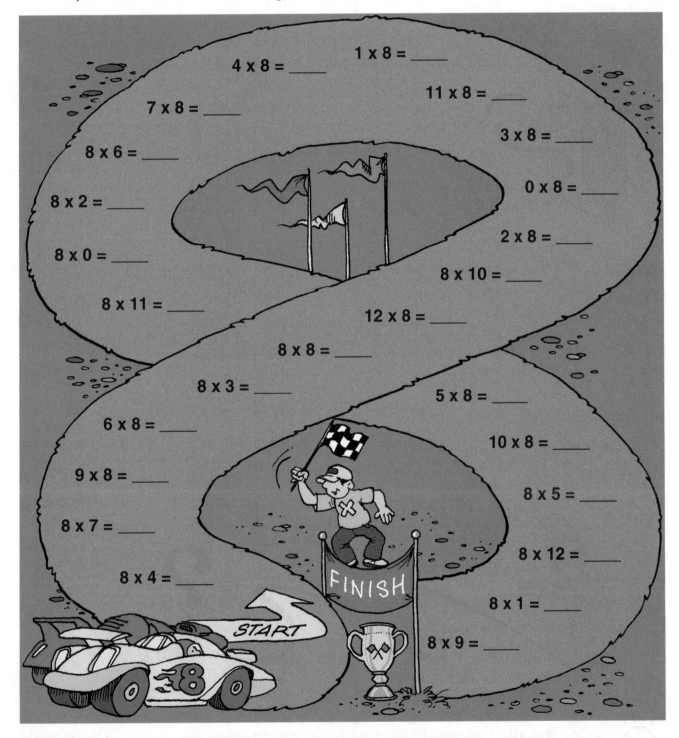

4 x 8 = _____

1 x 8 = _____

7 x 8 = _____

11 x 8 = _____

8 x 6 = _____

3 x 8 = _____

8 x 2 = _____

0 x 8 = _____

8 x 0 = _____

2 x 8 = _____

8 x 11 = _____

8 x 10 = _____

12 x 8 = _____

8 x 8 = _____

8 x 3 = _____

5 x 8 = _____

6 x 8 = _____

10 x 8 = _____

9 x 8 = _____

8 x 5 = _____

8 x 7 = _____

8 x 12 = _____

8 x 4 = _____

8 x 1 = _____

8 x 9 = _____

 **Racing Ricardo rapidly raced 8 times around the Eight Track. It took him 12 seconds to rapidly race one time around the track. How many seconds did it take him to complete the race?**

# Cross-Number Puzzle

Multiply. Write the number word for each product in the puzzle. Don't forget the hyphens!

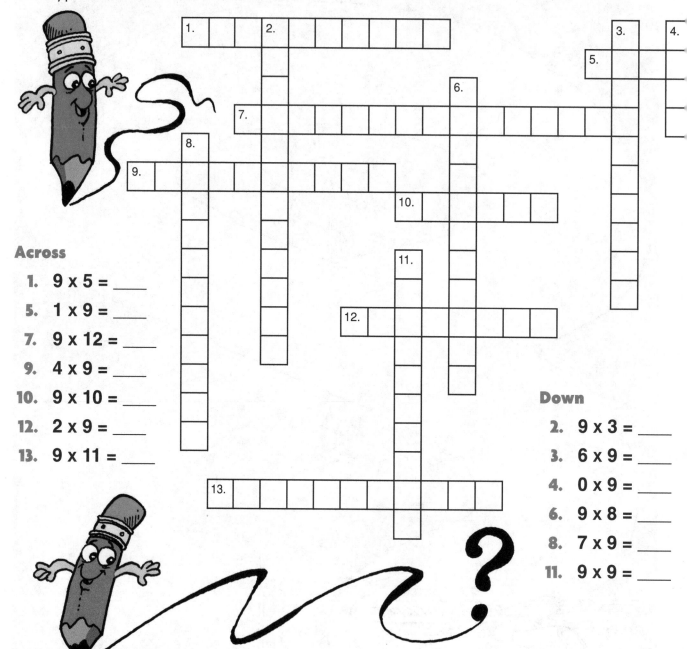

## Across

1. 9 x 5 = _____
5. 1 x 9 = _____
7. 9 x 12 = _____
9. 4 x 9 = _____
10. 9 x 10 = _____
12. 2 x 9 = _____
13. 9 x 11 = _____

## Down

2. 9 x 3 = _____
3. 6 x 9 = _____
4. 0 x 9 = _____
6. 9 x 8 = _____
8. 7 x 9 = _____
11. 9 x 9 = _____

 **Justin just finished putting together a puzzle of a castle and wants to know how many pieces are in the puzzle. He knows he put together nine pieces every five minutes. If Justin worked for one hour, how many pieces does the puzzle have?**

# Around Town

Multiply.

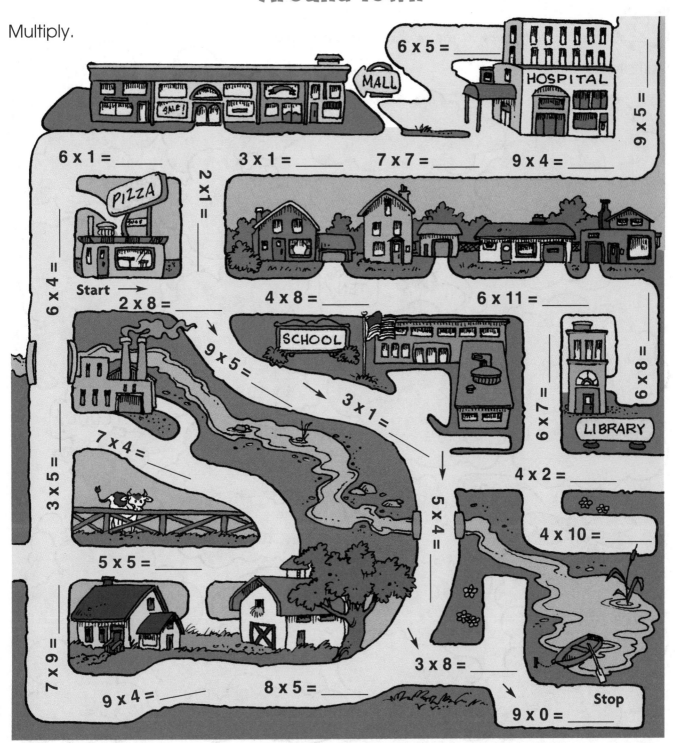

6 x 5 = _____

9 x 5 = _____

6 x 1 = _____   3 x 1 = _____   7 x 7 = _____   9 x 4 = _____

2 x1 = _____

6 x 4 = _____

Start →

2 x 8 = _____   4 x 8 = _____   6 x 11 = _____

9 x 5 = _____

3 x 1 = _____

6 x 7 = _____   6 x 8 = _____

4 x 2 = _____

3 x 5 = _____

7 x 4 = _____

5 x 4 = _____

4 x 10 = _____

5 x 5 = _____

7 x 9 = _____

3 x 8 = _____

Stop

9 x 4 = _____   8 x 5 = _____   9 x 0 = _____

 After finishing three slices of pizza at the restaurant, James walked to the pond to meet his dad. James and his dad were going to go canoeing. Add the products on the road James walked along from the pizza restaurant to the pond. Follow the arrows. What multiplication fact has a product equal to this sum?

# Cloud Ten

When multiplying by 10, the product always ends in 0.

Multiply.

7 x 10 = _____

10 x 0 = _____

10 x 9 = _____

1 x 10 = _____

3 x 10 = _____

9 x 10 = _____

10 x 5 = _____

10 x 8 = _____

HANG TEN!

10 x 2 = _____

10 x 4 = _____

10 x 3 = _____

10 x 10 = _____

8 x 10 = _____

6 x 10 = _____

WAY COOL!

0 x 10 = _____

4 x 10 = _____

COOL!

10 x 7 = _____

11 x 10 = _____

10 x 1 = _____

10 x 12 = _____

10 x 10 = _____

2 x 10 = _____

10 x 11 = _____

12 x 10 = _____

5 x 10 = _____

10 x 6 = _____

Every morning Miranda chooses her favorite ten clouds in the sky. She especially likes clouds that look like animals. If Miranda does this every morning for a week, how many clouds will she choose altogether?

# Eleven! Eleven!

*When multiplying the factor 11 by a number from 1 to 9, double the number to find the product.*

*Examples: 11 x 5 = 55      11 x 7 = 77*

Look at each multiplication sentence. If the product is correct, circle it. If the product is incorrect, cross it out and write the correct product above it.

8 x 11 = 81

3 x 11 = 33

4 x 11 = 48

5 x 11 = 66

9 x 11 = 99

11 x 6 = 66

2 x 11 = 22

7 x 11 = 74

1 x 11 = 12

6 x 11 = 54

11 x 2 = 21

11 x 3 = 23

11 x 8 = 88

11 x 5 = 55

FINE DINING

11 x 4 = 44          11 x 9 = 88          11 x 1 = 11

# Thinking Thoughts of Twelve

Write a multiplication fact in each box using 12 as a factor for the product on each wastebasket. Use a different sentence for each product.

**A.**

84   0

**B.**

96   132   72   144   36

**C.**

12   60   84   108   48

**D.**

120   48   96   132   24

Elizabeth wrote 12 different multiplication sentences on each of 6 different pieces of paper. After solving all the problems, she discovered 5 of the problems had the same product. On another piece of paper, show how many multiplication sentences Elizabeth wrote in all. Then write 5 multiplication sentences with the same product.

# There Are No Obstacles Too Big for You!

Use a stopwatch to time how long it takes to multiply around the obstacle course.

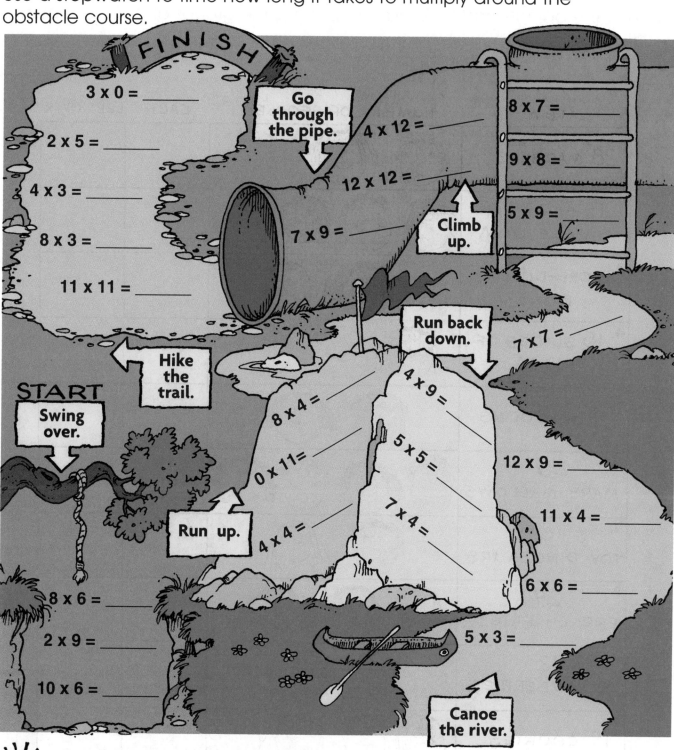

FINISH

3 x 0 = _____

2 x 5 = _____

4 x 3 = _____

8 x 3 = _____

11 x 11 = _____

**Go through the pipe.**

4 x 12 = _____

12 x 12 = _____

7 x 9 = _____

8 x 7 = _____

9 x 8 = _____

5 x 9 = _____

**Climb up.**

**Run back down.**

7 x 7 = _____

**Hike the trail.**

8 x 4 = _____

0 x 11 = _____

4 x 4 = _____

4 x 9 = _____

5 x 5 = _____

7 x 4 = _____

12 x 9 = _____

11 x 4 = _____

6 x 6 = _____

START

**Swing over.**

**Run up.**

8 x 6 = _____

2 x 9 = _____

10 x 6 = _____

5 x 3 = _____

**Canoe the river.**

**In the morning, four students completed the obstacle course. In the afternoon, five students completed the same course. If each student completed the course seven times, how many times altogether was the course completed?**

# Eager Seeker

Divide the objects and food equally among the groups of people shown below. How many will each person receive? How much will be left over?

| ITEM | NUMBER OF PEOPLE | EACH | LEFT OVER |
|---|---|---|---|
| 1. 28 MARBLES | | | |
| 2. 15 STICKS OF BUBBLE GUM | | | |
| 3. 8 ONE-DOLLAR BILLS | | | |
| 4. 15 SLICES OF PIZZA | | | |
| 5. 4 BALLOONS | | | |
| 6. 25 MARSHMALLOWS | | | |
| 7. 6 TOY DINOSAURS | | | |
| 8. 29 FRENCH FRIES | | | |
| 9. 12 STRAWBERRIES | | | |
| 10. 19 COOKIES | | | |

# Animal Caller

A bar graph shows information. This bar graph shows the speeds of animals in miles per hour. Use the graph to answer the questions.

WHICH ANIMAL IS...

1. THE FASTEST?

_____

2. THE SLOWEST?

_____

3. GOING 40 mph?

_____

4. 20 mph FASTER THAN A CAT?

_____

5. HOW MANY 4-FOOTED ANIMALS ARE LISTED?

_____

DO THE BARS SHOW...

6. ANIMAL NAMES AND mph?

_____

7. SPEED OR WEIGHT?

_____

8. INFORMATION ABOUT TIGERS?

_____

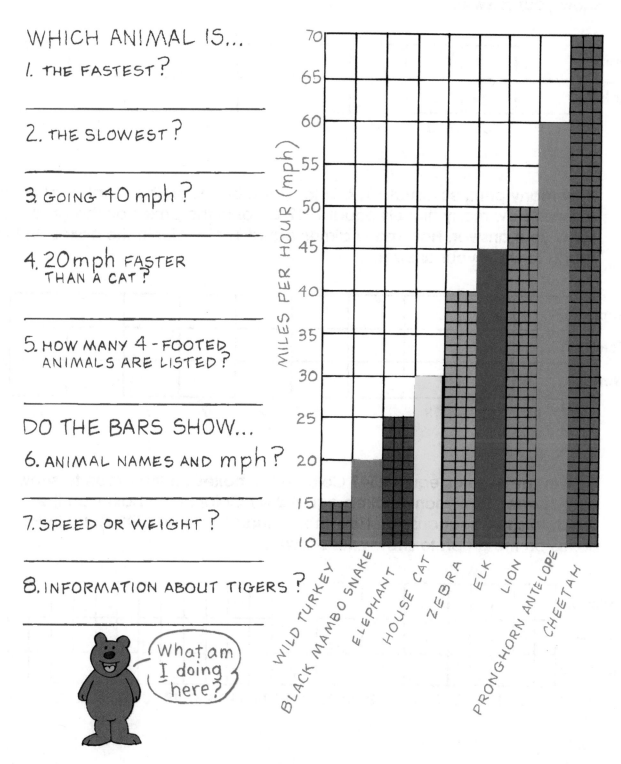

What am I doing here?

# Great Graphing

How many pennies equal 5¢? Color in the boxes on the graph to show your answer. How many nickels equal 5¢? Color in the boxes on the graph to show your answer.

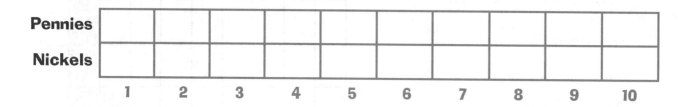

**Pennies**

**Nickels**

1   2   3   4   5   6   7   8   9   10

How many pennies equal 10¢? Color in the boxes on the graph to show your answer. How many nickels equal 10¢? Color in the boxes on the graph to show your answer. How many dimes equal 10¢? Color in the boxes on the graph to show your answer.

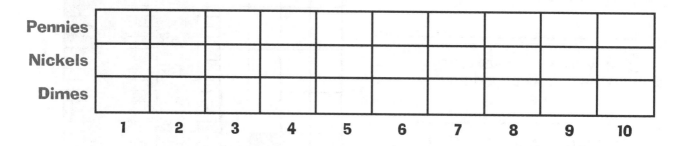

**Pennies**

**Nickels**

**Dimes**

1   2   3   4   5   6   7   8   9   10

How many pennies equal 25¢? Color in the boxes on the graph to show your answer. How many nickels equal 25¢? Color in the boxes on the graph to show your answer. How many quarters equal 25¢? Color in the boxes on the graph to show your answer.

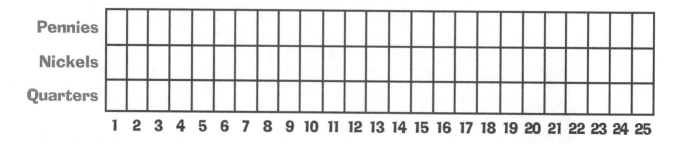

**Pennies**

**Nickels**

**Quarters**

1  2  3  4  5  6  7  8  9  10  11  12  13  14  15  16  17  18  19  20  21  22  23  24  25

# Graph Drafter

A line graph shows how something changes over time. This line graph shows temperature changes during a year in New York City. Use the graph to answer the questions below.

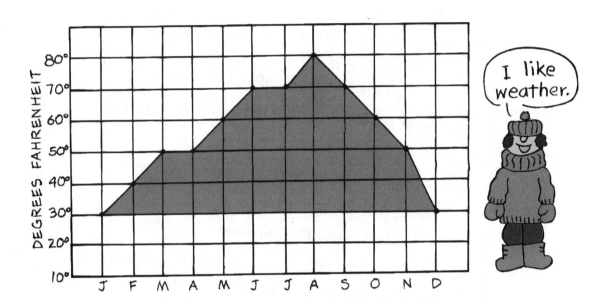

SUGGESTION: SHORTEN THE NAMES, LIKE JAN, FEB, AUG, SEP, OCT, NOV.

1. WHAT 2 MONTHS WERE THE COLDEST? _____

2. WHAT WAS THE TEMPERATURE OF THE HOTTEST MONTH? _____

3. WHAT MONTHS WERE 70°? _____

4. ANY TEMPERATURE CHANGE BETWEEN JAN. AND FEB.? _____

5. WAS THE TEMPERATURE EVER WARMER THAN AUGUST? _____

6. DID IT BECOME COLDER OR WARMER IN JUNE? _____

7. DID THE TEMPERATURE RISE OR FALL IN OCTOBER? _____

8. WHAT MONTH IS THE 5th MONTH? _____

9. HOW MANY DEGREES BETWEEN 40° AND 80°? _____

# Goody for Fractions!

Wash your hands, then gather the recipe ingredients and equipment listed below. To prepare the peanut butter–oatmeal drops, simply mix the ingredients together, roll the dough into balls, and place the balls on the wax paper. Chill the finished drops for about an hour, then enjoy your tasty "fractions" with family or friends!

---

### NO-BAKE PEANUT BUTTER–OATMEAL DROPS
(makes about 30 1-inch drops)

cup peanut butter (smooth or crunchy)

cup corn syrup

cup confectioner's sugar

cup powdered milk

cup uncooked oatmeal

Mix all the ingredients together. Roll into balls. Chill for about one hour. Then eat!

---

Now try these fraction pictures. Can you write the fraction each picture shows?

1. 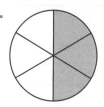  _____

2. 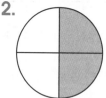  _____

3. 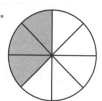  _____

4. 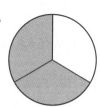  _____

5. 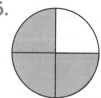  _____

6. 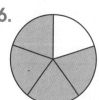  _____

7. 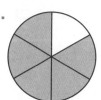  _____

8. 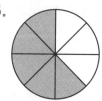  _____

# Flower Shop Fractions

Choose 2 colors for each bunch of flowers. Color some of the flowers one color. Color the rest of the flowers the other color. Write a fraction to tell how many flowers there are of each color.

1.

$\dfrac{\phantom{0}}{8}$ are ▢

$\dfrac{\phantom{0}}{8}$ are ▢

2.

$\dfrac{\phantom{0}}{6}$ are ▢

$\dfrac{\phantom{0}}{6}$ are ▢

3.

$\dfrac{\phantom{0}}{5}$ are ▢

$\dfrac{\phantom{0}}{5}$ are ▢

# Into Infinity

Solve the problems. Then rename the answers in simplest terms.

If the answer is $\frac{1}{4}$, $\frac{1}{8}$, or $\frac{1}{16}$, color the shape purple.

If the answer is $\frac{1}{2}$, $\frac{1}{3}$, or $\frac{1}{7}$, color the shape blue.

If the answers $\frac{2}{3}$, $\frac{3}{4}$, or $\frac{7}{8}$, color the shape green.

If the answer is $\frac{3}{5}$, $\frac{4}{5}$, or $\frac{5}{7}$, color the shape yellow.

If the answer is $\frac{9}{10}$ or $\frac{11}{12}$, color the shape red.

Finish the design by coloring the other shapes with colors of your choice.

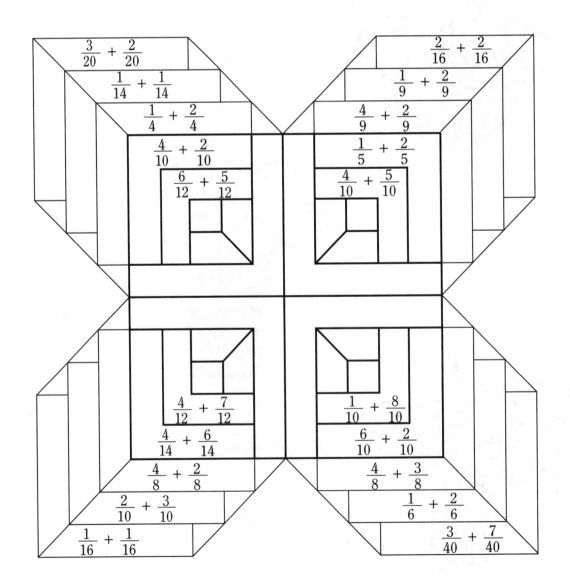

# Time for a Riddle!

Read the riddle. To find the answer, find the clock face that matches the time written under each blank line. Then write the letter under that clock face on the blank line.

**Riddle: What did the little hand on the clock say to the big hand?**

Answer.  "___  ___  ___  ___      ___  ___  ___
            10:00   3:30   3:30   6:05      2:25   3:45   6:15

___  ___      ___  ___  ___  ___ !"
4:45   6:05      2:55   3:45   3:45   2:55

O          U          E          N

T          Y          M          A

# Fact Finder

Numbers can be used to count and to measure. Complete the measures below by writing how many are in each.

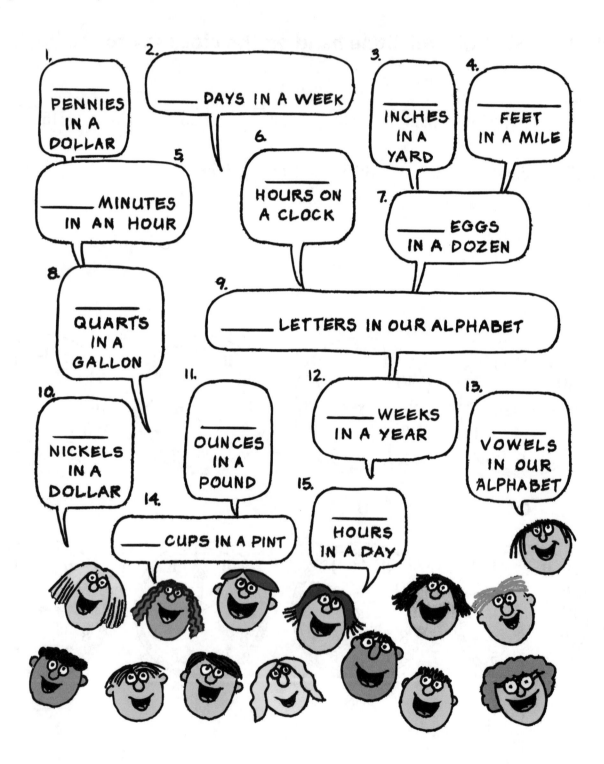

1. _____ PENNIES IN A DOLLAR

2. _____ DAYS IN A WEEK

3. _____ INCHES IN A YARD

4. _____ FEET IN A MILE

5. _____ MINUTES IN AN HOUR

6. _____ HOURS ON A CLOCK

7. _____ EGGS IN A DOZEN

8. _____ QUARTS IN A GALLON

9. _____ LETTERS IN OUR ALPHABET

10. _____ NICKELS IN A DOLLAR

11. _____ OUNCES IN A POUND

12. _____ WEEKS IN A YEAR

13. _____ VOWELS IN OUR ALPHABET

14. _____ CUPS IN A PINT

15. _____ HOURS IN A DAY

# Amount Counter

How many triangles and squares can you count in these geometric figures?

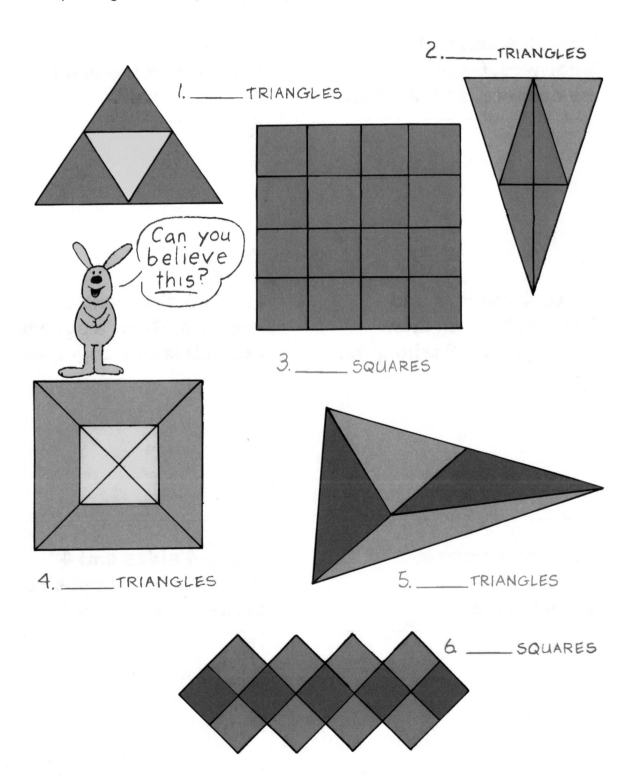

1. _____ TRIANGLES

2. _____ TRIANGLES

3. _____ SQUARES

Can you believe this?

4. _____ TRIANGLES

5. _____ TRIANGLES

6. _____ SQUARES

# Riddle Teller

Read the riddle. Then draw the shape it describes.

**I have 3 sides and
3 corners. One of
my corners is at the top.**

1.

**I have no corners.
One half of me is like
the other half.**

2.

**I have 4 corners and
4 sides. You can draw
me by joining 2 triangles.**

3.

**I have 5 sides and 5
corners. Draw a square
and a triangle together.**

4.

**I am not a square,
but I have 4 sides
and 4 corners.**

5.

**I have 4 sides and 4
corners. My 2 opposite
sides are slanted.**

6.

# Pattern Block Design

How many total pieces are in this pattern block design?

2 + 2 + 2 + 4 = _____

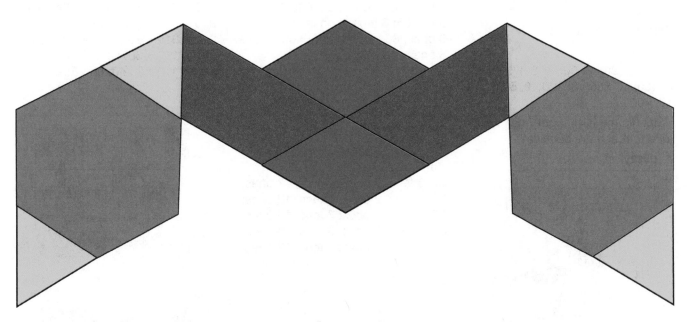

Now make your own design. Use 10 pattern blocks different from those used above. Cut out the shapes and trace or glue them in the space below. You may need to use a shape more than once.

Write an equation to show how many of each shape you used.

Equation: _____

# Answer Key

**Page 5**

Answers will vary.

**Page 6**

A. thousands;  B. tens;  C. hundreds;
D. tens  E. hundreds;  F. ones;
G. tens

Riddle answer: a secret

**Page 7**

1. 10;  2. 20;  3. 50;  4. 90;  5. 200
6. 400;  7. 600;  8. 300;  9. 500;
10. 700

What did the farmer get when he tried to reach the beehive?

A "buzzy" signal

**Page 8**

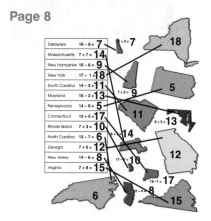

**Page 9**

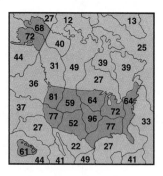

**Page 10**

Check that the child has circled the correct number of stars. 3 tens, 4 ones, 34; 4 tens, 5 ones, 45; 2 tens, 7 ones, 27; 7 tens, 0 ones, 70; 5 tens, 3 ones, 53; 6 tens, 5 ones, 65; 3 tens, 6 ones, 36; 8 tens, 0 ones, 80; 13, 13 + 50 = 63, 6 tens, 3 ones

**Page 11**

52, 53, 82, 61, 96, 52, 82, LINCOLN; 37, 83, 42, 42, 83, 78, 64, 96, 82, JEFFERSON; 98, 72, 64, 65, 53, 82, 45, 47, 96, 82, WASHINGTON

**Page 12**

37: 3 tens, 7 ones; 2 tens, 17 ones;
52: 5 tens, 2 ones; 4 tens, 12 ones;
85: 8 tens, 5 ones; 7 tens, 15 ones;
43: 4 tens, 3 ones; 3 tens, 13 ones;
68: 6 tens, 8 ones; 5 tens, 18 ones;
26: 2 tens, 6 ones; 1 ten, 16 ones

**Page 13**

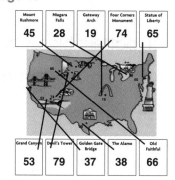

**Page 14**

S. 75; I. 24; A. 65; R. 38;
R. 84; W. 57; H. 58; I. 64;
U. 33; O. 72; L. 51; M. 34;
B. 71; L. 80; G. 69; U. 48; WILLIAM BURROUGHS

**Page 15**

324 + 632 = 956; 241 + 551 = 792;
155 + 331 = 486; 213 + 313 = 526;
415 + 322 = 737; 143 + 146 = 289;
202 + 216 = 418; 431 + 422 = 853;
142 + 233 = 375; 541 + 134 = 675;
335 + 333 = 668; 712 + 232 = 944;
220 + 314 = 534; 514 + 334 = 848;
224 + 143 = 367; 416 + 132 = 548;
Joe brought $5.40, and Ellie brought $4.35.

**Page 16**

| 954 | 427 | 554 |
|-----|-----|-----|
| 684 | 349 | 364 |
| 945 | 844 | 472 |
| 457 | 574 | 942 |
| 473 | 424 | 842 |

| 970 | 373 | 872 |
|-----|-----|-----|
| 723 | 577 | 884 |
| 507 | 476 | 397 |
| 743 | 771 | 712 |
| 575 | 674 | 974 |

**Page 17**

| 574 | 534 | 558 |
|-----|-----|-----|
| 346 | 506 | 763 |
| 852 | 523 | 945 |
| 952 | 524 | 965 |
| 897 | 563 | 723 |

| 726 | 622 | 923 |
|-----|-----|-----|
| 327 | 288 | 525 |
| 628 | 824 | 431 |
| 826 | 842 | 428 |
| 724 | 725 | 527 |

**Page 18**

534 − 275 = 259; 467 − 278 = 189;
392 − 296 = 96; 625 − 366 = 259;
988 − 589 = 399; 735 − 367 = 368;
854 − 397 = 457; 564 − 498 = 66;
339 − 249 = 90

**Page 19**

A. 496 − 188 = 308;
B. 956 − 668 = 288;
C. 547 + 239 = 786;
D. 379 + 345 = 724;
E. 723 − 162 = 561;
F. 422 − 215 = 207;
G. 957 − 688 = 269;
H. 884 + 834 = 1,718;
I. 956 − 578 = 378

## Page 20

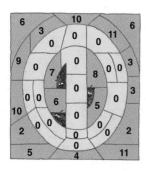

## Page 21
A. 6, 16, 22, 14; B. 16, 8, 4, 8; C. 24, 10, 20, 24; D. 18, 2, 20, 14; E. 0, 12, 6, 0; F. 10, 18; G. 12, 2; H. 22, 4; Rhymes will vary.

## Page 22

3, 30 letters

## Page 23

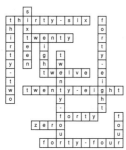

44 buttons

## Page 24
A. 10; B. 1; C. 7; D. 50; E. 12; F. 30; G. 11; H. 15; I. 40; J. 9; K. 5; L. 5; M. 35; N. 60; O. 4; 60 nuts

## Page 25
yellow: 0 + 66 + 12 + 60 = 138; red: 18 + 30 + 36 + 6 + 24 = 114; orange: 54 + 18 + 66 + 24 + 30 + 48 = 240; blue: 42 + 72 + 60 + 24 = 198; green: 30 + 42 + 48 + 72 + 0 = 192; purple: 36 + 18 + 12 + 18 + 6 = 90; 48 fireworks

## Page 26

49 times

## Page 27
32, 56, 72, 48, 24, 64, 96, 80, 16, 0, 24, 88, 8, 32, 56, 48, 16, 0, 88, 40, 80, 40, 96, 8, 72; 96 seconds

## Page 28

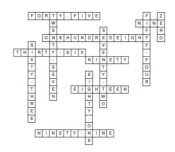

108 pieces

## Page 29

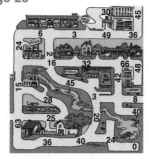

12 x 9 = 108

## Page 30

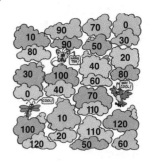

70 clouds

## Page 31

## Page 32
A. 12 x 7 = 84, 12 x 0 = 0; B. 12 x 8 = 96, 12 x 11 = 132, 12 x 6 = 72, 12 x 12 = 144, 12 x 3 = 36; C. 12 x 1 = 12, 12 x 5 = 60, 7 x 12 = 84, 12 x 9 = 108, 12 x 4 = 48; D. 12 x 10 = 120, 4 x 12 = 48, 8 x 12 = 96, 11 x 12 = 132, 2 x 12 = 24; 72 sentences; Answers will vary.

## Page 33

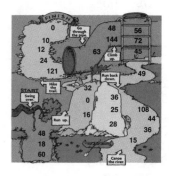

9 x 7 = 63

## Page 34
1. 9 R1;  2. 3 R3;  3. 4 R0;  4. 5 R0;
5. 2 R0;  6. 6 R1;  7. 3 R0;  8. 9 R2;
9. 6 R0;  10. 4 R3

## Page 35
1. cheetah;  2. wild turkey;  3. zebra;
4. lion;  5. 7;  6. yes;  7. speed;  8. no

## Page 36
5 pennies equal 5 cents, one nickel equals 5 cents

10 pennies equal 10 cents, 2 nickels equal 10 cents, one dime equals 10 cents

25 pennies equal 25 cents, 5 nickels equal 25 cents, one quarter equals 25 cents

## Page 37
1. January and December;  2. 80°;
3. June, July, and September;
4. Yes; 10°;  5. No;  6. Warmer;
7. Fall;  8. May;  9. 40 degrees

## Page 38
1. 3/6;  2. 2/4;  3. 3/8;  4. 2/3;
5. 3/4;  6. 4/5;  7. 5/6;  8. 5/8

## Page 39
Answers will vary.

## Page 40
3/20 + 2/20 = 1/4
2/16 + 2/16 = 1/4
1/14 + 1/14 = 1/7
1/9 + 2/9 = 1/3
1/4 + 2/4 = 3/4
4/9 + 2/9 = 2/3
4/10 + 2/10 = 3/5
1/5 + 2/5 = 3/5
6/12 + 5/12 = 11/12
4/10 + 5/10 = 9/10
4/12 + 7/12 = 11/12
1/10 + 8/10 = 9/10
4/14 + 6/14 = 5/7
6/10 + 2/10 = 4/5
4/8 + 2/8 = 3/4
4/8 + 3/8 = 7/8
2/10 + 3/10 = 1/2
1/6 + 2/6 = 1/2
1/16 + 1/16 = 1/8
3/40 + 7/40 = 1/4

## Page 41
Answer: "Meet you at noon!"

## Page 42
1. 100;  2. 7;  3. 36;  4. 5,280;
5. 60;  6. 12;  7. 12;  8. 4;  9. 26;
10. 20;  11. 16;  12. 52;  13. 5;
14. 2;  15. 24

## Page 43
1. 5;  2. 11;  3. 30;  4. 16;  5. 8;
6. 17

## Page 44

## Page 45
10; Pattern block designs will vary.